Where in the World is SUMMER

*This book is a special dedication to our precious baby girl, Summer.
The joy we've experienced during your first year fills our hearts with excitement
for the many beautiful years yet to come.*

We Love You!

Copyright © 2023 Shanley Simpson

All rights reserved. No part of this publication may be reproduced, distributed, or transmitted in any form or by any means, including photocopying, recording, or other electronic or mechanical methods, without the prior written permission of the publisher, except in the case of brief quotations embodied in critical reviews and certain other noncommercial uses permitted by copyright law. For permission requests, write to the publisher, addressed "Attention: Permissions Coordinator," at the address below.

Print ISBN: 978-1-63616-163-1

Published & Illustarted By Opportune Independent Publishing Company
Info@opportunepublishing.com

Use this QR code to add to Summer's college fund!

At the Cuban beach, toes kissed the sand; Summer splashed in waves, hand in hand.

Sun kissed her cheeks, wind tousled her hair. In Cuba, she found joy beyond compare.

Next, in Florida, a party so sweet, a "Sip and See," they called it. Oh, what a treat!

Summer met kin, smiles all around. In heels, she stood on newfound ground.

In Chicago, she ventured to a baby spa,
cucumbers on eyes and a bubble bath... ooh la la!
Pampered while nails being painted and filed.
In the water, she splashed; her spirit ran wild.

All close in age, a joyful and lively meet,
together they made memories, a bond complete.

To Mexico's lagoon her steps did trace,
a new world opened, a smile on her face.

Crystal waters shimmered beneath the sun's warm clutch. In Mexico's tender arms, she found joy oh, so much.

Jamaica marked her passport's final stamped place, a land of beauty with a heritage to trace.

Meeting more family, hearts pure and bright, in the land of reggae, her world felt just right.

A year of adventures, so vast and grand.
All happened before she could count to one on her hand.

Remember this tale of Summer's first year,
with adventures galore and laughter so clear.
There's so much more to come, you'll see,
as she shares her journey with you and me.

Summer Nova Simpson was born on Nov. 17, 2022, to Sean and Shanley Simpson in Dallas, Texas. From day one, she was a bright-eyed beauty! She hit every milestone right on time; some she even did early. Summer loves music and dancing, but smiling most of all. She's a fast learner who has mastered eating solids, waving, and traveling (quietly) on planes. Summer has visited five countries and tried 100 foods all within her first year of life.

She enjoys FaceTiming with family, spending time with friends and watching Little Baby Bum on YouTube. She has plans to learn more exciting things and can't wait to see what adventures await her as a one-year-old.